Unwrapping E

Exploring Emotional Excursions from Emptiness to Euphoria

Erica Alyse Holton

Unwrapping E
ISBN (Trade pbk.)
978-0692765647

Cover and Interior Art: E. A. Holton
Layout: Chris Massenburg
Cover Design: Fuze Aquene Namid
http://www.istimyouleye.com/

HPJ's Writeeasy Publishing
Durham, North Carolina

There are some literary moments when the reader feels the poetry being read…and then there are those unique experiences when the words actually feel the reader; and the so privileged reader knows it. Erica or simply "E" manages to pull something special off in her writing style. Like Zora Neale Hurston or Sonia Sanchez, her poetic expressions come across as personal; filled of wisdom; and easily flowing with self-reflection…not only for the writer, but for the reader as well. It almost feels as though we wrote the poem ourselves…or at least we were there when the point of inspiration occurred. Simply, E's words are true, gifted, sweet, warm, caring and real…significant of the phrase that so describes her as "a poet's poet."
- Aquene Namid, Sirius~A (Fuze)

E' is a writer that gives you her heart and soul in each poem. You believe in the poems because you know she has been through things, survived and kept going just like so many of us. There is a lot of personality in her writing. It makes her work familiar and touching. I am sure you will find there is no one like E'.
- Dasan Ahanu

Everybody and their mama is a poet from so many angles, views and stations. However, there are rare ones that come along and command your eyes to listen with such little effort. They grab you by the hand and walk you through their journey, have you feeling like you went on an escapade from life. The poet's poets are the ones we turn to to get refueled. That's Erica, that breeze, that sunshine, that refreshing rain to cover a well needed cry. I embrace her gift and I'm honored to share her vision. Love Ya Queen…
- Antonio R. Diamond (Tone)

E' shares, bears and reveals herself completely within her work and words. I've had the pleasure of being part of her journey and have personally benefitted from the positive energy and synergy she creates.
- Nicole L. Beckwith (Nick)

To have been able to watch the evolution of this sister, my kindred spirit, on the mic has been amazing and to have the opportunity to read her journey captured in ink is just captivating! Thank you E' for sharing ALL of you with all of us.
- Elizabeth Santana Almeida*Simply Poetic (Liz)

Erica, my dear friend, you've invigorated the fundamental philosophy of alchemy as you trans-mutate our everyday language into that, which is nothing short of ethereal. I'm in awe of the manner in which you inspire those beckoned by your cadence to be lifted and invited to soar in formation with the like-minded. Your passion serves to expose the magic and beauty in language while allowing the listener and/or the reader to escape the daily hustle and nestle in the embrace of your divine gift. The space between this moment and what's in store for your future is pregnant with the burgeoning actualization of the poet within. I'm pacing the halls fully aware of every sound above a whisper as I await the arrival of your full set of gifts that will overtake what's on the outside. I can't wait to see what you name her... The integration of the inside and the outside as a whole new self is born to save us from mundane in the form of much awaited Wednesday night.
- C. Garner, Sr. (Cliff)

Thoughts flowing

Imagination growing

Mind releasing

Peace increasing

Stress fleeing

...all thanks to pen & paper

Love travels an interesting journey in our lives and no person is immune to the inevitable bumps. We all have been bruised and scarred. We all have tried to find the emergency button to get off. But hope is the safety bar. Forgiveness is the seatbelt and desire for happiness is the gravitational pull that keeps us seated.

Close your eyes.
Let's ride together.
LIFE~

ℰ

Unwrapping E'

Table of Contents

HUMBLY BROKEN

WHERE NOW

Where now?
I let the tears fall as I looked in the mirror and saw an unrecognizable face. Where had my smile gone? I saw before me an image full of pain from the disappointments and ills of life.
Broken
Resentment had long ago set in changing who I really was. This act of being "ok" grew tiresome...this act that I had it all together. I thought about it all, my future, my decisions, my life as I knew it to be.
Got in the shower, the water simply merged with the falling tears.
Stepped out, unchanged.
Turned off the light. Made no difference.
Cried in the dark.
Where now?
It took years for me to learn.
The question: Where do you go?
The answer: UP!!

BLOWING

The wind took my lover like a leaf~

And blew him into the clouds~

And I followed as it danced across the sky, being lifted
and tossed…kissing tops of trees, tip toeing fields,
swirling around butterflies.

And I watch and wait for the descent, so I can run and be
there when it lands with gentle hands and a warm smile.

But while I watch it in the sunlight, my eyes burn
GREATLY!!!

NO THANKS!!

Thanks, but no thanks. Imma keep mine hot, black, strong and straight.

Had one too many that dipped their spoon into my cup and changed my outlook. Were you thinking I needed an additive? Were you trying to soften me, cool me, alter me, lighten me?

I don't mind enhancements of some sort but I allowed more than flavoring. I allowed you to change me...when it was not necessary. I am what I am which was more than enough. But in this world of long lash extensions, push up bras, eye color changing surgeries, corset type contraptions, lace fronts, fake backs, "the reals of Hollywood," the internet, magazine covers, air brushed up people.... In a world of changing faces, switching places, multiple phases, complex races, hardly left a trace of self. I fell into some funk thinking I needed to be something different. I needed to be changed by you so I could accommodate what you were used to.

I did that... I allowed that... Had amaretto, french vanilla, caramel macchiato, eggnog latte, ginger hot bread, hazelnut, cinnamon and pumpkin pie spice...and everything nice...and when I was feeling a bit frisky around the holidays I even tried chocolate chip mocha thin mint nuccccahhhhh!!!!

And at the bottom of the cup what was left was residue of you and none of me. When I looked in the mirror I wasn't sure who I'd see. So I had to undo, undress, purge and say "leave me be." I'm now happy, unaltered and amazingly free.

And if that doesn't fit your palate, put down the spoon, put down the cup and dip elsewhere cause it is what it is...AND I AM HOT, BLACK, STRONG AND STRAIGHT!!!!

BRANDY

She stays on your mind. I can tell by that faraway look in your eye. Many times we're together I know you're thinking of her.

The care you take.
The planning.

You make sure you see her every day and it makes me feel lonely. Even when you're trying to be attentive to me thoughts of her just seem to linger.

BRANDY

I, being in love with you, was willing to do anything to try and make this work between all of us. So every once in a while I'd join in. I indulged you both just to make YOU happy. The three of us would lay on the couch together, watch movies together, we took her to our bed. Licked her off your lips and I have to admit she tasted good to me but I'm not in love with her. I'd close my eyes and try not to watch or be bothered when you caressed her sometimes before me. I don't have that bond with her that you have.

BRANDY

This thing with her has crippled our relationship. I just wanna let go and let you two go off together walking happily in the sunset. However, I'm the stubborn one. I refuse to let go. I don't want her to have you. I'm tired of the threesomes. In fact, her very name now sickens me.

BRANDY, BRANDY, BRANDY

I watch how you hold her. Your fingers are tight and I find myself jealous, envying the love you have for her.

I wish I was that bottle!

THE SHIT

When I met you, you seemed legit
You seemed to have it together
Like you were "Mister It"
Your confidence HAD confidence
It was holding its dick
And I liked that persona
Cause you CAME with it
A strong man, a strong mind
Come, let's talk a bit
I liked what I saw
I must admit
Your words were so smooth
Made me forget
To watch your actions
Caught up in your wit
Soon I peeled back your layers
To see if with me you'd fit
And I found evidence
That did not transmit
You portrayed one thing
But you did omit
Flaws upon flaws
And lies your tongue spit
You cracked like glass
Needed an emergency kit
Cause you bled your truths
Your veins they split
Now I'm looking at you wobbly
I've got to sit
Cause I fell for the picture
And all that came with it

Baby, go see a doctor
And do this real quick
A prescription for blue pills
You should now go get
Cause your "game" is on point
But your spirit, limp as shit!

IF I GIVE UP

If I give up on us understand what I've already done to get there.

I've already run into the night without a coat for protection, without a hat or gloves or umbrella or boots. I ran out to save us from the storm.

I've already jumped onto the highway stopping cars, blocking trucks, buses, bikes, pedestrians - making them wait and detour so that we could pass by easily on our journey.

I've already climbed the trees, crawled to the roof, jumped from the airplane to catch stars to light our way when there was darkness.

I've already run out in front of you and threw myself down stretching my arms, legs, neck, even my fingertips, scratching, reaching to create a bridge so that you could cross my back over to comfort.

I've already run through sand, jumped into the ocean without a boat, without a sail, without a paddle, without a life jacket, without fear, with only one mission - to save us.

I've already sprinted across the earth jumped down pressing my hands onto the chest of the body, recalling the appropriate resuscitating steps in my mind pressing, counting, waiting, pressing, counting, waiting, pressing, counting, praying in order to revive us.

So if I give up...IF I GIVE UP...IF I GIVE UP understand where I had been and what I had to do...the agony and how it pained me. If I give up understand all that happened before I got there. Because I never, ever wanted to give up!

REMEMBER ME

You jokingly said you needed some Ginkgo Biloba.

But in your sporadic chatty conversations I've learned so much about you. You remember your pin numbers, your codes to unlock your phone, other secret files you keep there, and your passwords to ALL your e-mail addresses. You remember what year the movie *Friday*, *Next Friday* and *Friday After Next* came out. You remember the exact make, model, color and year your favorite muscle dream car was when you were twelve. You remember all your nephew's birthdays. You remember who won the Heisman Trophy for the last ten years easy. You remember your high school sweetheart's telephone number even now 25 years later. You know your social security number, driver's license number, and plate number for your car and truck. You remember what day, month and year Prince came out with your beloved *Black Album...* You remember all your frat brothers' line names...You, you even remember the lock combination from your locker in middle school....

...but you can't remember to call me.

VAMPIRES

My heart is what convinced me to let you in. Your words, your presence made me grin. It grew and grew was a lovely start. Before I knew it you had my heart. In the beginning, all was well. How it ended I could never tell. I kept giving, you kept taking...gave and gave...now heart is breaking. The clear imbalance was sucking me dry...had me feeling like I was bout to die. When you left thought my life would end. Moved back my locs, saw bites on my skin. My energy, my words, my love, my time sifting out to your spirit from mine. As years passed I would see that you were not really for me. And I do know that God has a plan. He is grooming me for a better man. All is not gloomy, all is not lost, But chile I do now carry some garlic and a cross.

To ward off...the vampires!!!!

HOPE RESTORED

RIPEN

I was a raisin
Dried up
Sunbaked
Weather-beaten
Exhausted
Spent

Then you~

Today, I smile
Energized
Ignited
Excited
Full

Now a muscadine

STAR GAZING

Quiet, cold night
Clear, cloudless horizon
Tight embrace

Conversations flowed as we looked to the sky for
answers about our future but we got sidetracked by the
stellar beauty above us.

Our eyes and fingers drifted as we studied the
stars...North Star, 7 Sisters, Big Dipper, contemplating
planets, planes and sparkly things...Realizing that life
and love are bigger than the small space we take up.

What is life without love?

Nothingness.
Void
Without light

I was content in your arms as I watched and mapped the
stars but I turned to you and saw what made me smile
more. For it was not the stars but the twinkle in your eyes
as you watched me!

BORING

I wanna be boring. I wanna do boring stuff with you.

Could tell you I dream of you throwing me the keys to a brand new car like the Lexus commercials they show at Christmas, big red bow on top. I hug you and run out of our 5,000 square foot home and jump for joy at my new toy!

Could tell you that I dream of finding airline tickets left on my Egyptian cotton pillowcase. A trip to Bermuda planned by you to surprise me for my birthday. 5 days, 4 nights...all inclusive trip paid for; Not financed; Not planned for months; Just a quick trip to see me smile.

Could tell you that I dream of the weekly spa treatments you spoil me with or the $60 steaks from my favorite restaurant on date nights or the salsa dancing lessons we enjoy together.

But I...I just wanna be boring with you.

I wanna warm up leftovers for us and talk to you about the weather forecast for the next seven days.

Wanna lay on the couch with you and not really pay attention to that sitcom you love but I dislike, just to hear you chuckle.

I wanna sit on our bed and paint my fingernails while you're reading a book and the room is quiet for hours.

I just wanna be boring. Ya know.

I wanna curl up in your lap when I have cramps and I'm too uncomfortable to bend to kiss your fingers when you rub my tummy.

Wanna talk to you about football while I'm filling up the sea salt shaker in our kitchen. I wanna sort clothes for washing while you're shaving...wanna sit on that rickety chair in the garage while you vacuum the cars...wanna see who has double coupons this week...Harris Teeter, Kroger, Lowes, Food Lion...wanna mop the floor while you dust the piano.

I wanna do the mundane, routine, mindless, drab, lame things with you...because being boring with you is the most exciting, amazing, exhilarating, mind blowing thing I could ever dream of...because…it's with YOU!

And you, you make the "nothings" by which I base my "everything" on...just…just cause it's you!

~Dedicated to Shawn Certain ~

THE STALKER

He watched
Deciding on the right time
Patiently waiting
Stalking
Calculating every move
Observing
Noticing everything
Surveying
Memorizing the plan
Anxiously anticipating
Ready to pounce on his victim
Then he stepped out
Like a thief in the night
With meticulous moves
Creeping
Sneaking
Crawling
Prowling
He came
Uninvited
Unannounced
And stole
My heart!

INSOMNIA

Late nights
Early mornings
Midday
Sunsets
Rising sun
Half past the hour
Dinnertime
High tide
Low tide
Bedtime
Brunch
Early starts
Midnight thoughts
Insomnia - mind always on you!

SPELL ON YOU

I put a spell on you~

I put a spell on you with the things I say,
the things I know,
the things I'll do
I put a spell on you!

No four leaf clover,
no chicken feet,
No concoctions to make you dream
of me when you sleep
No pee in your cup with liquor that cheap!

I put a spell on you.

No flashing lights to confuse your eyes
No voodoo doll for your heart's demise
No grand presentation that's full of lies
No ice in my mouth to suck your dick
No potions in your stew to make you shit
No, No, No, No...Baby, that ain't it

I put a spell on you.

No sitting on your lap to grind you slow
No itty, bitty shorts so my ass cheeks show
No see through shirt that hangs real low
No sign that says "I'm easy, let's go"
No fake fertilizer to make your feelings grow

But I put a spell on you.

Not using thick hips, round boobs, loc'd hair, soft
lips...Tattoos down my back and a dimple in my smile.
I've got all those but that ain't my style
Gonna put something on you to make ya stay awhile

I...I...I put a spell...

Gonna use something that's unheard of today
No need to even touch you as you pass my way
This spell has no fumes, no smoke
no claws from birds
All Imma do is use nouns, adjectives and verbs
I'm gonna gain your heart...just using my words...

I put a spell on you!!

THE APOLOGY

Yesterday we were human-

We are people who have been shaped by our experiences from many years of living. People who are gifted in verbalizing our views and thoughts about these experiences. People who are passionate about the words we use to describe those views.

And yesterday we were human-

The very thing that causes the magnetic bond between us caused us to crash and it fractured us. The strength that usually is united ended up on different sides of the court and WE showed up. The you and the me; the ones we have fallen in love with, respect and admire; the passion, will and need to express moved from being side by side to eye to eye. We were human.

And you, the protector, showed up, honoring your views, exhibiting self, feeling the need to express, wrapped in ways and wanting to protect me from myself and from my views. But I, your equal, need and want no protection from anyone. I have my own perspective, my own lenses that sometimes differ from yours. Me, I am courageous enough to protect my truths as though they were my children. WE happened and we growled and showed incisors cutting in our own realities and we bled, both wounded a bit, went to our own corners and settled like shaken glitter in a jar and the residue that was left was STILL us.

Would I choose you not to be the very thing that I adore the most? To not be the very thing that causes my heart to flutter when I think of you? But could I ever not be who I was meant to be? - The woman, spirit and soul that has made a place of home in your heart, the tower that you sometimes lean on, would you alter me? NO!

Yesterday we were human and we quarreled.

And today the sun shown his lovely face again
A new day.
Another day and we yet still are captured, catapulted and captivated, connected by our humanities but caught by our individualities!

And we live yet another day in love.

I'm sorry.

LOVE BLOSSOMS

BIRTH

Was as if I labored, belly swollen, contractions, tussling with anticipation. Had been fooled earlier by false beliefs of being ready. Yet I knew that this was really it. The timing was now!!

I held on through the pains and trauma of life. What was about to be delivered would cause me to forget all previous woes. And after much time when all was in sync I gave birth...to love...to you!

Took one look at you, heard your voice just once and knew that your entrance had changed my life. We see the world through the same lenses, speak the same language, you are new but old... Your spirit mirrors mine so much that I can't tell us apart. So you MUST have come from me and I from you.

Now that you're here it is as if you impregnated me with your seed and I turned and delivered you. As if our souls keep overlaying and we keep finding each other more everyday through each other...as if you're turning into me and I you. As if we were one spirit and some cosmic collision separated us and we have been trying to find the other.

But now you are here; We are back to self – oneness; We have given birth to love!

MY HEART'S HEART

My heart had been roughed up, jacked up
Held up by the throat, punched in the stomach
and dropped like dead weight by the ills of love
Giving too much, trying too much
Expecting much and being disappointed much
And when it landed it was as if the last breath was
knocked out
Slumped in the corner, left for dead

And I being a great actor went along my way
Convincing others I was fine
Convincing self that I didn't need the heart
I didn't need to feel

I didn't need love

So my heart slowly regained consciousness
Finally picked itself up from the alley it was left in
Limping along, holding on to the walls around it to
steady itself
Putting one foot in front of the other
Hobbled along to safety
Slowly breathing
Getting stronger, healing
Until the wounds were less visible

And we went about our way
My mind and body in one place
And my heart along for the ride
Only needing to transport blood to organs to rise in the
morning

And many came along
Asking the heart to come out, venture out, trust again
but the heart refused being weighed down by memories.
Many suitors came along offering their hand and their
promises

But the heart gracefully declined saying it was too busy
taking care of the body

And then you
You came along
Convincing the mind and the body that the heart had
other functions
It really was made to give itself away
And the heart looked at you Shawn, took a deep breath,
closed its eyes and gave you its hand

You gave my heart back its heart
And taught us to believe in love

LOVE

Love wakes up and says today I owe you all of me. Says yesterday is gone...left with last night's darkness. I'm obliged anew. I dedicate myself once again with the rising sun and morning dew.

Love says today I choose you.

Love says let me be your bridge from here to there...where "there" lies sweet, peaceful skies and a swinging hammock that rocks me ever so gently...when life is good and I hum the same songs as the birds in the trees BUT "here" feels like woaaaaahhhh, dry, burning coals weighing on my soul and my head is too heavy to hold. Love says crawl on my back and I will carry you to the other side. Hold tightly to me.

I'm strong enough for us both. Trust in me.

Love says when all else is stripped away and you're just you...when no one else is looking and you're naked, happy, ugly, kind, mean, strong, weak...when your spirits are high and when they are crushed...when you are bleeding, blinded, broken and bombarded by life you are still beautiful to me because I accept all parts of you.

You are more than enough.

And if the attempted eloquence is not received in the manner that it is given and your mind just needs simplicity...

Love says "NUCCAH, I GOT YOUR BACK!!! KNOW THAT!!!!"

GOOD SLEEP

Exhausted

After you

After I

After we finished

Drank my wine

Laid in your arms

On your chest

Snuggled under

Your chin

Enveloped

Sharing your air

Breathing in sync

With you

Following the rhythm

Of your heartbeat

Laid there

Thirty minutes

Before I slept

In heaven

CUP OF LOVE

I wake and witness of all the miracles that happen with each sunrise. The wonder fills me from fingertip to fingertip and I am flooded yet again with emotion. It throws me in a cup of love that I stew in all day and there is where I find you.

YOU ARE MY UNIVERSE

Just as the earth revolves around the sun, my smile deepens as it revolves around you. Though I am whole, happy and at peace in my own celestial being this collision that took place in my life because of your entrance made broad the joy that I carry within.

Just as the moon has a gravitational pull on the ocean waves, your being, your spirit, the essence of who you are has a hold and tug on me that is unmistakable and unbreakable.

And when we are apart, though my world keeps spinning on its own axis, it is as if there's an eclipse blocking complete light that radiates from your love. I find my hands constantly outstretched trying to reach for your energy force because without you a black hole looms...

And even with the ebbs and flows of this sometimes tough life that shakes us both you are indeed my universe.

I am _certain_ that you are mine!

<u>BLOOM</u>

Close my eyes
I breathe you in
You radiate through my soul
You oxygenate, resuscitate, pollinate
my flowers
and allow me to bloom
and show my true colors.
Your love
gives life!!!!

Intermission begins...

Lover's Haiku
without a compass
no map to help me return
I'm lost in his kiss

Funny Haiku
Little girl takes walk
Swiper the Fox is stalking
Quick, call the police

Dating Haiku
Peeked the resume'
He had plenty to offer
Still he was a jerk

Life Haiku
Despite fame, fortune
All experience life's woes
No pillow stays dry

Poet Haiku
Poet pollinates
Transfers the words from her soul
Drops them from her lips

Intimate Haiku
Use senses with rest
Better than watching him sleep
Hearing his heartbeat

Shawn's Haiku
He's my Iron Man
His "strong" made me respect but
His "weak" made me love

Summer Haiku
Sat upon the steps
Cars with heavy bass whiz by
Makes me want to dance

Grad School Haiku
Laughter and giggles
Brain fried from statistics work
Everything funny

Journey Haiku
Life like a river
It flows this way and that way
Just enjoy the trip

Reality Haiku

Life is all too short
Dropping petals on a grave
Brings back my focus

Strength Haiku

Rare and beautiful
Made strong by pressurized force
I am the diamond

Exercise Haiku

Danced with two left feet
No more Zumba class for me
But I'm back again

Photography Haiku

Black and white photos
Show depth and definition
Are most colorful

War Haiku

Battles are like pearls
Combined, shows beauty and strength
Alone, may get lost

Teenage Haiku
Hormones out of whack
She's saying I make her sick
But she wants a hug

Stripper Haiku
Audience of one
Let me be sexy for you
Go get your dollars

Emotional Haiku
The mic doesn't lie
The words I say are strong talk
But my voice quivers

Image Haiku
Life sometimes scars us
The blemish is beautiful
Stronger we become

Relationship Haiku
Together we grow
Focus should be on other
Not the mirror

Vulnerable Haiku
I love you right now
I loved you yesterday too
Even when I cried

Reality Haiku
In church all my life
Know that God is in control
At times I'm still scared

His Haiku (S.C.)
Should call you coffee
Strong, grounded and smell so good
You wake up my spirit

Acceptance Haiku
At times dreams come true
Though wrapped in different paper
The gift still wondrous

Shallow Haiku
Beautiful inside
She focuses on her shell
Wasting Energy

Intermission ends...

DESIRE AWAKENS

67 MINUTES

He called before he came. I heard his car pull up from my bedroom. I had been sitting, waiting. 20 minutes earlier I was in the shower, shaving my legs, lotioning my body and applying lip gloss. He was stunning and I blushed when I saw his face. And when he crossed the threshold of my door I knew he would give me all I wanted. He kissed my forehead and placed his keys, his wallet and his phone on the piano and he took me in close to him for a slow, careful dance to a love song that hummed through the speakers. He stopped, looked down at me and gave me the softest brush on my lips with his...and then again...and then again ...and then again until my chest beat heavily through my shirt.

And for the next 67 minutes we made love like there was no tomorrow. We played as if on a see saw on a playground, like a spinning top on a hardwood floor...like never ending crashing waves upon a shore, my body like the San Andreas Fault. Experienced an earthquake and continuous tremors due to seismic waves and kinetic energy and he feasted like he was starving from every orifice on my body and I returned the favor.

It was beautiful!

The stuffed animal sitting in the corner covered his eyes and blushed at what he had witnessed. And no part of the bed was jealous because we covered each corner...We abused and challenged each nut and bolt that held my headboard together.

And when we finished we were drooling, dragging, dripping, drained, drenched, drunk and drop dead tired, drowning in ecstasy. I felt myself in slow motion hit my pillow...and I laid back to catch my breath, to slow my heart rate and racing pulse. I laid there and closed my eyes after having amazing, dirty, kinky, hair pulling, nasty, shit talking, naughty, mind blowing sex

But I thought of you.

And in that instant, in that moment I knew as he laid sleeping lightly beside me that I was still in love with you!

IT

On the nightstand many square, open packages, ruffled sheets and discarded clothes gave evidence that we had done **IT.**

Your tongue tasting like me, my skin smelling like yours, your sweat falling beneath you, our bodies pressed closely together, you kissing my vine from end to end and me holding the perfect posture so you could go deeper to experience more of **IT.**

And I drifted off in your arms, my hair invaded your face, your legs intertwined with mine;
You held me tightly as we took naps losing consciousness between our sessions.

And in the morning I stood in front of you as you sat on the bed. There was silence between us as we took in the night before when it happened again and again and again many times. We smiled because we knew we had made passionate love but we had also done **IT.**

We~

Involved Trust

Interchanged Teachings

Imparted Truths

Influenced Tranquility

Inspired Transformation

Initiated Testimonies and

Intersected Time with

Insatiable Treasures and

Intimate Touch

We had done **IT.**

CANDY CANE

She needed it
That feeling overwhelmed her. A sweat, a heat, a
haunting. She needed it.

As in a trance...got up...closed her office door, turned on
the music. Sat back in the chair, laid back, got
comfortable, listened to the jazz. Placed one black,
leather boot on her desk, the other remained in place;
picked up the candy cane left in her mailbox by co-
workers.

Slowly removed the plastic wrapping
Breath quickened
Heart rate, pulse racing
She needed it - a release
Had been a tense week

Slipped down the black lace that covered her thighs
Adjusted
Body ready
Unbuttoned her blouse
Lightly purred

With two fingers
Inserted the candy cane inside her body
Moved it in and out...slowly
Her walls thickened with the increased blood flow
Moved the candy quicker
Quicker
Quicker
She needed it. Ohhhhhh

Until she and the candy became one
As the feelings intensified
Climax
Ahhhhhhh
Laid back
Back arched
Opened her eyes
Removed the candy
Left her body smelling like mint, now eating the candy,
which tasted like her.

KISS ME

He kissed me and took me away
Strangled my tongue with his sweetness
Intertwined my soul with his until we became one
Lost myself and found myself in his kiss

In that kiss we journeyed to Zimbabwe
Zaire
Zululand
Zion
Zanzibar and
New Zealand

Played in waterfalls in the deserts
Slid down guitar strings
Had a sword fight with fresh blades of grass
Sat upon tops of trees and watched the fireworks in
January
Caught shooting stars and placed them in our pockets
And then went swimming in the glass of green iced tea
on the table

In his kiss
Saw the sunrise, set and slumber
Closed my eyes and visited 28 planets not known to man

Within his kiss
I rose and fell
Upon his back I climbed, chirped, chimed and shined
In time I wrote this rhyme
And then whined for more

I lived for his kiss
I died for his kiss

Kiss me fool
Kiss me...

WATER THE ROSE

I am the flower
You, the hose
Nourish me plenty
Water the rose
I shall not stop
Stand, let it unfold
Unfold, unravel
Better yet unleash
I'm here to learn
Also to teach
Close your eyes
while I get on my knees
Relax, relax
I'm ready to please
Unzip, unbuckle
Look down at my face
Slow and melodic
Then I pick up the pace
Passion intense
So you spill your seed
I shall not move
Til all I've received
Your soul to mine
Blending all things
Honored to serve
you as the king...
All I'd do to see you smile
Take you to heaven for a lil while.

DAYDREAMING

Work quiet
People off
Office empty
Outside, rain
White noise humming
Atmosphere soothing
Mind drifting
On you
On us
Thoughts recalled
Remembering times
Your entrance
Phones tossed
World unplugged
Lights dimmed
Time frozen
You approach
Stepping closer
Lips tremble
Intimate touch
Close quarters
Skirt unzipped
Blouse unbuttoned
Bra unhooked
Locs loosened
Heels remain
Tongues dancing
Body aroused
Yours erect
Fingers moving
Grabbing muscles

Nipples hard
Breathing erratic
Walls filling
Blood rushing
Body warm
Body ready
Wetness present
Hearts synced
Pillows moved
Covers thrown
Thighs opened
Head lowered
You feasted
I wasted
No time
Climax looming
Waves crashing
You stopped
Adjusted direction
Turned over
My body
Assumed position
Stomach down
Legs spread
Breathing labored
Trust required
Entrance taken
Motion slow
Entered there
Forbidden places
Exotic traces
High stimulation
Innocence taken

Mind racing
Pain, pleasure
Wrapped together
You growing
I'm coming
I'm coming
Then again
Then again
~~~
SOMEONE CALLING?
PHONE RINGING!
EYES OPEN
FOCUS BLURRY
DREAM INTERRUPTED
STILL WORKING
AT DESK

DAMN!!!!!!!!!

LIFE PROCEEDS

REFLECTION ON MAY 10, 2016

16,790 days upon the earth
18 years in Roanoke Rapids
5 years in Greensboro
23 years in Raleigh
3 proms
30 months of wearing braces
3 years as a school bus driver
88 keys on a piano
42 years of sitting at the same piano
5 years at A&T State University
3 of those years partying
1 year partying a little less
1 extra year BECAUSE of the other years partying

25 years in the field of contracts
4 different organizations
17 consistent years at a non-profit
7 years there without a raise
18 months of grad school
3.93 GPA in grad school
14 first years of life with natural hair
Next 26 years putting creamy crack relaxers in my hair

6 years back to natural
104 locs upon my head
14 years of marriage before divorce
3 children
2 C-sections
1 vaginal birth
1 summer spent in Liberia, West Africa

8 friends that I still keep in contact with there

1 diagnosis that changed my life

37 treatments of radiation
4 oncology doctors
25 pounds lost since last summer
10 more to go

636 intentional Facebook friends
20 that know me well
12 that can tell you my thoughts by looking at me

9 that will go to their grave with my secrets

8 tattoos on my body
7 pairs of black leather boots
6 holes in my ears
5 other members of my beloved City Soul Cafe team

4 chambers of the heart broken 3 times
2 hands to touch the face of the love of my life
and 1 mouth to thank God for it all.

SEARCHING

We all just want to be understood. To feel validated, like we make a difference, like we're noticed, like we're more than enough, like there is something in us that makes somebody else's heart flicker. At the end of the day we are all searching to be loved.

We are all searching for truth in eyes that we behold dear even if we see doubt, anger, hurt and pain. Whatever it is, we want truth and transparency. We have been hurt by others who have masked their identities and motives because they couldn't face their own fears. They've played games with our unsuspecting hearts. We want to give sincerely to someone who will accept us as is but more importantly we want to find those who are willing to say "Here am I. I too am flawed but this is MY truth". WE would happily embrace them.

We are all searching for that giant shade tree in our lives, the place where we can run to for shelter from the storms, from the heat and problems that sometimes pellet us like hail. We all desire to have that place that restores us, revives us, realigns us, protects us. We all want that safe space where we can take off our day and close our eyes in relief...breathing deeply and exhaling slowly, the place that oxygenizes our spirit.

We are all searching for our path laid out before our birth. The stars were perfectly aligned at the specific time we entered this world. We have not only dreams to dream but to chase down and capture. We have intersections to cross and those encounters will catapult

---

us to higher heights once we take hold of the lessons. We will grow when we finally accept the teachings. Our life is out there. Our ancestors are there. God is there. All there, all watching us scramble around on hands and knees in our darkness. We just have to stand and remove the blinders because they know, just like I know, that we are all searching.

BOY BYE

He broke my stride; Made eye contact, grinned and
introduced himself, extended his hand, showed me his
watch, monogrammed cuff links and pointed out his car,
certain that I'd be impressed. Told me where he went to
grad school, his fraternity name and informed me that he
held the title of Vice President …said he had a three-car
garage house that needed the company of a beautiful
girl…said he was from Philly (by way of Zebulon).
Assured that I was captivated by his resume he then
asked with his arrogant ass "and where might you be
from?"

And I replied:

Me? Well, I, I am from Him that made the wind and
directs the waves
I am from Egyptian royalty whose pictures live in caves
I am from steep rapids from the Roanoke River banks
and from ancestors whose blood and spirit I give and
owe many thanks
Men and women of the land, mighty hands, sturdy
backs, strong wills
From a lineage of strength and wisdom, visionaries of the
fields
I am from the dreams that visit me when I sleep
And the words that spill from my pen from long hours
that I keep
I am augmented chords that flow from my piano keys
And from results of many loved ones being diligently on
their knees

I am from a place where life issues sometimes spread like cancer
And travel on a magic carpet where God has had the answer
I am the fragrance of perfection and hue of wondrous light
I stand on faith and promises and depend upon God's height
I am from peace, from music, from art, from flying birds above
I am the center of the heart and extend my hands with love!

I turned around and that nuccah was gone...he won't ready!

Boy bye!

WONDER WOMAN IS TIRED

Mind busy
Thoughts heavy
Body spent
Gaze low
Breathing erratic
Anxiety rising
Rest needed
Comfort Desired

Craving security for my spirit. The cares of the world
have me depleted as I have spilled my energy on
countless situations that needed my touch. And I do
them all willingly, cheerfully, fixing all around
me...holding up pillars for lives that are not my own.

The super and the wonder in the woman slowly draining,
seeping like drips of water. I feel my strength just wane a
bit...considered the story of a weary soul that touched
Jesus as He was passing by and He stopped asking who
had touched Him because He could feel healing power
being released. And I imagine the releasing of that
power would make Him even greater. But I am not Jesus.
I'm a mere mortal and I keep being touched and touched
and touched and touched and I can feel all of me
draining.

Those I've upheld are busy trying to get themselves
together and I am happy as I see them pick up their
pieces, honored if I was even a small instrument or
vessel in their recovery from the pitfalls of life...but I
looked in the mirror and I saw eyes not quite as bright

and I'm smart enough, strong enough, wise enough to say to self "you need solid rest". But where are they. I want to shout "Come and see about me. Bring me a hammock for my cares, a pillow for my thoughts and time to heal and to rejuvenate! Care for me as I have cared for you."

Because Wonder Woman is tired!

GO

Step, step
Step
Push door open
Walk off porch
Cut across grass
Run...Run
Keep running
Out or breath
Go
Keep going
Get to safety
Run more
Run away
Until you can't go further
Stop
Wipe tears
Catch breath
Fall on knees
Grab the earth
Lay on ground
Call on ancestors
For strength
Look at sky, clouds
Close eyes
Listen to birds
To the wind
Hear squirrels playing
Bugs scrambling
Lay there
Think of the ocean
Calm self

Lay
Outstretched
To get peace
Stay there
As long as needed
For sanity

THE COMET

He came and stayed but for a moment
Sharing his light and his love
And left his mark all too soon
Leaving me breathless
I mourned the loss but was grateful for the encounter

Though the body is gone
Fragments of his precious life remain
Life unseen particles floating behind its path

And I just happened to be in the right place and the right
time to witness the crossing

LUCKY ME!

He moved swiftly through this earthly space – But left a trail
of memories with u...like a comet...No telescope is needed
to see that force traveling towards its rightful owner

He left a tail of memories with us like a comet

~Dedicated to Odell Clanton, Perry
Jones and William "Reese" Rush, may
you rest in perfect peace. ~

LIVE ON THE WILD SIDE

Smell the sunshine
Embrace the full moon
Taste the breaking waves
Hear the grass grow
Dance with the butterflies
Fly with the hurricane
Listen to the April showers
See the wind blow
Eat the words in a sonnet
Get lost in an ant farm
Become the sunset
Feel the dolphins swim
Slide down the cat's tail
Visualize the playing children
Bask in the thunderstorm
Visit Neptune on the weekend
Run fingers through the morning dew
Sift between the pink ocean sands
Climb Jacob's ladder
Ride the tidal wave
Jump off the top of a pyramid
Snooze on a baboon's back
Hug the trees
And live

MY PIANO

I was four years old when my dad brought her home. I was amazed. I stared. Was mesmerized but I'm sure I brought no intimidation to her. We became inseparable. When my eyes opened in the mornings I ran in her room ready. And many times after my appointed bedtime I'd sneak and try to quietly engage her. I couldn't wait.

And over the years she has seen so much like when I lost in the spelling bee contest in the 3rd grade pissed that I forgot to put the "b" in the word "doubt" knowing it's silent but I, too eager to answer, misspoke and I lost. I sat and cried. I placed my fingers on her to tell her. She already knew and as always was waiting there for me.

And in the 10th grade when the girls in my high school decided to have a secret "in group" that I wasn't privileged to be a part because of the particular blend from my mom and dad. My mother with her Cherokee Indian decent being very fair with coal black straight hair and my father rich in dark chocolate gave me my perfect hue. But I wasn't yellow. I was brown, too brown for this group. And though I said I didn't care that I was excluded, in my head I said, "fuck them bitches" when I sat down and told her I cried because of the rejection. She let me cry and start again and start again and start again.

And three years ago when a UNC doctor called me with test results and he said Erica Alyse Holton and cancer in the same sentence I froze for 48 straight hours. When I thawed I ran to her. My family and friends prayed and stayed by my side and I certainly shared my feelings with them but I told her the most. When I had surgery and through 33 treatments of radiation, which burnt my skin, I went to her daily and shared the song "Great is Your Mercy." To this day I can't get through this song because of the happy tears that fall. I am happy because cancer was the worst thing and best thing and I am sooooo grateful to be alive and well. It's because of her that I can be happy when I share this.

See it's something about her...my piano...something about the feeling I get when I run my fingers across those 88 keys. We've bonded for 40 years...she's never too tired, never opinionated. She listens. We work well together. She understands and gives me back all I give her.

Proms, headaches, heartaches, good grades, horrible grades, augmented chords, fragmented phrases, first dates, last dates, blind dates, key of D, sharps, flats, hospital visits, Beethoven, missing curfews, falling in like... In love...in hate, Mozart, ragtime, oncology appointments, disappointments, happiness, new jobs, promotions, divorce, lyrics, octaves. They all are woven together and they spill out of my fingertips when I sit at her feet...we make melodies together. Ultimately, we make love - My piano!

And now days shy of my 46th birthday I see this man and I like him. I like him a lot and he stays on my mind though he might not know it. And I wonder if knowing him has any potential of going anywhere. Just liking him is scary and the thought of future love with anyone is almost paralyzing because see I've given my heart out before just for a person to trample on it and abuse it. And it took me a minute but I got it together.   Patched it up and now I'm good but I have had these thoughts that I may possibly put my heart his hands if this blossoms.

But this keeps me up at night. Though I could think about if he'll bend down and let me touch his skin in my fingers; If his lips are as soft as they look; If I can go to sleep on his chest and wake up and he still be there; If I can interlock my fingers with his if we make love; if we will ever sit on a bed at 5am and talk about our dreams. I can think about all of that. But what I REALLY think about; The constant theme, the reoccurring dream, the unforeseen, this thing that keeps me up at night is.... After I've gotten to really know him, after the dust settles and if by chance he's still around and I take inventory of what he brings to my life. I sit and think of him and wonder JUST WHAT TYPE OF TUNE WILL I PLAY ON MY PIANO BECAUSE OF HIM!

RAIN

Their beautiful voices lull me to sleep, they calm my breathing, they seem to understand my cares.

I peer out smiling.

They came like carolers singing at Christmas. I stare and my heartbeat slows. Sopranos carrying the melody, altos harmonizing. Feels so familiar like treasured friends who share a lifetime of memories.

The clouds announce their coming arrival...laid the red carpet out for the grand presentation. They knew I'd be waiting, needing their therapy. I couldn't work, couldn't concentrate, couldn't think anticipating what their freshness would do my mind. Give me anew.

And I saw one, then another and another and I knew their entire choir was about to sing to me. So I placed my hands on the window to join in.

Rain.

JUST E'

She likes the sound of piano keys, ocean waves, reggae music and cloudy days. She likes the smell of lavender fields, soft pillows and pillow talk. She loves God, family, basketball, Redskins, neo soul, locs and tattoos, dancing, singing, writing, thinking, poetry, kisses and new Nike shoes!

She sometimes grabs a pen at 3am to capture thoughts, visions, words. Speaking to those who will hear. Sometimes brought to tears by the sheer fact that she has overcome, is overcoming, becoming all that was laid out before her birth...becoming daily anew, becoming love, becoming truth, becoming truth, becoming laughter, becoming light.

She's seen loss on so many levels. So, so many she'll never tell...still looks to the heavens and speaks to Odell. Staring at the ink residing on her wrist as a permanent reminder of the love truly missed.

Sometimes alone, resting quietly with a book, sometimes soaking up vitamin D. Other times needing to share her soul, Liz, Cliff, Shea, Nicole. Laughing hard sometimes her sides hurt, smiling at times trying to hide hurt brought on by those she trusted, cared for, loved...but that's life and she overstands that.

Sometimes she undresses and sees extra here and there. When she's naked and bare and bears a scar as a reminder that being a good person doesn't shield one from life, struggles, need, cancer, pain, questions, strife

---

and unanswered requests.   But then she looks closer bypassing all the flaws and sees a genuine smile, in spite, despite and it's all crystal clear.   Everything, all of it, is relevant, all important, all essential, all necessary for E' to be E' and she is completely happy with the reflection staring back at her.

I WEPT

I lay there motionless
Still, in silence
Uninterrupted
Uninhibited
Staring up at the ceiling
Without much care, in no discomfort, in no distress;
Totally relaxed, at ease, at peace with the world.

Then my mind wandered and I contemplated about
others lying in that same state, those who lay in that
identical position, flat on their backs
What were they thinking?
Where were their minds?

The woman who lay in a hospital bed bandaged from
head to toe, what was she thinking as she lay there
stationary just as I? Did any visions come to her head
about the truck that crashed into her Mazda on that rainy
Monday night eight weeks prior? Did she think of the
bones still stuck in her arms? Were her thoughts of her
child and her husband who sat by her hospital bed daily
or were they on the intoxicated driver who walked away
from the scene unharmed? What was she thinking as she
lay on her back just as I?

Or the child who lay in bed staring hopelessly at his
ceiling, clutching his covers, trying not to see the scary
images coming at him every time he dared to peek. His
older sister told him that those monsters would surely
come on the day he thought they'd forgotten about him.
Did he wonder how the creatures would pull his teeth

out one by one just as his sister had promised? Were his thoughts of the terrifying monsters that hid in his room or the sister who slept peacefully in the next? What were his thoughts, as he lay there motionless just as I?

What were her thoughts? The little girl who visited her grandparents every summer. The little girl who adored the farm but hated the sight of one person in that house. What did she think of on Friday nights after her uncle went out and played pool with his friends, then stumbled in through the side door? He'd creep into her room, pounce upon her, lift her nightgown, cover her mouth and force himself inside of her. What did she think as she lay there unable to speak, unable to move? What were her thoughts as he whispered to her how he'd cut her throat with the same blade that he slit the chickens in the barn if she were to utter a word. What could she be feeling? Where was her mind? Where was her soul? Where was God, as she lay immobile on her back as I?

What about the mother lying ready to deliver her baby? What were her thoughts? Did she imagine her child 18 years later entering an Ivy League school? Did she imagine this child becoming a great doctor much like the ones racing up and down the halls outside her door? Or did she think about the one bedroom apartment that she shared with her sister and three nieces? Did she think about the expense that this child would bring and the incredible way her life would change and how much more cramped the apartment would be with another body living there...another mouth to feed? Would this child be healthy? Would it need special attention? Could she be a good mother? Could she learn to love, could she learn to care though the baby's father denied his participation? What were her thoughts as she lay there thinking about the big unknown as a brand new life lay within her wrestling about?

The old man, laid there, eyes fixed on the bright sunshine that filled the sky after the afternoon spring shower, his pockets empty, his skin pale, his body dirty. What were his thoughts? Did he think of the two young men who grabbed him as he walked through the park on his way to the corner store? Did he think of the moment he felt the blow to his head? Did he think of the shovel they used to hit him to silence screams? Did he think of the $21.14 they took from his front pockets along with pictures in this wallet of his grandchildren who were waiting at home for ice cream from their papa? What were his thoughts before? He laid there dead for three full days, flat on his back, just as I?

I thought of all of them; I thought of the others that lay upon their backs and I wept. I wept. I wept for the anxious feelings about the unborn child about to come into a crowded world; for the young child's fear of monsters hiding in dark corners; for the silent pleas for help from a vulnerable little girl; for the woman's struggle to breathe and recover after a horrific car accident; for mourning grandchildren created by less than $25.00 taken by misguided boys in need of attention and I wept for the deceptive peace that accompanies the naïve feeling that all is right with the world as one lays upon their back to rest. I wept for those who do not have that gullible placidity and for those of us who do.

MY PRAYER

I, in my feeble, frail and weak capacity, cannot fathom the Greatness of God. God, who knows all about me; knows what I am thinking before the idea comes to my mind; knows what I will say before I part my lips to speak; knows everything I hear before I turn in the direction to listen; Thou, who knows what I will feel before a breeze has reached my skin; who knows how many tears I will cry before the water accumulates in the wells of my eyes; God, who knows all of this, all the time, about everyone.

I am not worthy to ask of anything. My requests seems miniature and frivolous when I look outside of my own predicament and see how others are struggling in their own; But God, in all of His grace and mercy, listens to me too. No matter how small my prayers are, He listens and answers. He knows even before I began to desire. He is there waiting for me to humble myself and commune with Him.

In all my days upon the Earth I will have praises upon my tongue for being in His presence. When sometimes I don't feel like being with myself, He is there. He is closer than my next breath. I, a simple sinner, will have an everlasting companion, who speaks when I have no words to say; who sees when my eyes are closed; who hears when I am too inflexible to listen; who solves the problem before I come to know that there is one.

God, who is an Omnipotent Spirit
God, who is unlimited in Power

God, who is the Creator of Miracles

God, who is accustomed to working outside of nature will be with me always. I shall never go without or be alone and I will thank Him always...for He is God alone!

USED

When I die I wanna be worn slam out.
Down to nothingness
Unrecognizable
Depleted...Gone

I wanna look like my grandmother's bible;
Like my dad's favorite pair of underwear;
Like my most comfortable gym shirt...like my aunt's back
bedroom mattress. I wanna be like that old
neighborhood dog.

My grandmother had this Bible that she kept by her side
all the time... And she wrote all in it...everywhere. The
spine was gone. The book was raggedy. I remember
when it was in two pieces but she would open that thing
up like she was parting the Red Sea. And after three cats,
a broken hip and a few more great grandchildren, the
book ended up being in way more sections than that.
She kept this rubber band around it. And one day I told
her... I said imma go get you a brand new bible and she
scolded me... "Don't need nothing new. That's what's
wrong with you young people...always wanting new.
This here Bible (now mind you missing most of 2nd
Timothy) has served me well".

I wanna serve well...

I'm grown now but when I was a teenager and stayed
with my parents I had chores.... Not for money.... For the
right to breathe.. And one was washing clothes, then
taking them OUTSIDE and putting them on the clothes

line in the back, back yard by the honeysuckle shrubs...Going back to get them, folding them up AND putting them away. And my father had this pair of underwear that I swear wasn't worthy enough to be a dust rag. It wasn't. I remember him taking a shower one day and shouting from his bedroom "where are all my clothes" cause I had taken THAT pair out. I was gonna throw them away but he shouted so loud that I just conveniently found them... And when I inquired about their importance he said "they're just comfortable Erica,"

I...I wanna bring comfort.

My grandmother had a lot of sisters and one of them was named Lydia... We called her Liddy. This woman looked exactly like Lena Horne...never got married, never had children. She kept her life still cause she was waiting for the perfect man to come along and she kept her house the same way all the time. Would upgrade NOTHING. And when my cousins and I got to fighting over who was the best basketball player amongst us she got tired...and would say "You two go in there to the front room, you two go sit on the porch and you (talking to me) you go back there and lay down in the back room cause no doubt you done got all these kids riled up with that feisty talk"... And she shouted and I don't wanna hear nothing outta your mouth bout my mattress. It's familiar. It makes me feel good now.

I want my presence to make somebody FEEL good.

It may be hard to believe (I'm being facetious) but I was born in the country and we had neighborhood dogs.

These animals had never seen a vet, the inside of a house nor a flea or tick collar. They miraculously lived off of everybody else but this particular dog people called Butch. He may have been a mutt but he was around when we played double dutch in the driveway standing guard, watching us. He was still around when we rode three wheelers up and down the dirt path. I almost ran over him when I was learning to drive a five speed when I was 14. I tell you I think he photo bombed one of my prom pictures. Then I didn't see him anymore and I asked my mom "You guys seen Butch? She said well no but he probably did like animals do, they go away when they know they're about to die. She said "He gave you kids his all".

See I wanna give my all.

When that bright light comes for me I wanna have nothing left...cause I wanna be useful, be used, be used up cause I wanna give it all away. Wanna keep nothing for self... Nothing!!!

See when I die I wanna be worn slam out
Down to nothingness
Unrecognizable
Depleted...Gone

And I start every morning with this in mind trying to give much away.

Starting with my smile.

To my parents, my brothers and sis,
my children, my niece and nephew
my poetry family and
to my Shawn!

I love you!
E.

A	S	J	H	G	S	L	Y	Z	X	T	H
G	K	O	R	R	H	O	N	D	A	P	U
E	M	Y	L	O	V	E	S	A	V	I	G
R	A	O	L	V	K	Q	H	E	I	E	S
A	R	U	C	A	D	I	A	B	E	C	N
R	T	S	O	P	J	D	W	W	R	E	K
D	E	M	O	R	G	A	N	K	F	S	I
F	V	C	O	U	R	T	N	E	Y	O	S
U	N	Z	M	C	A	G	H	I	J	F	S
E	R	I	C	A	N	L	M	X	G	E	E
V	G	N	A	R	T	H	E	L	L	V	S
C	I	T	Y	S	O	U	L	F	A	M	O